T0032876

ON THE CORNER OF
CHOCOLATE AVENUE

How Milton Hershey Brought Milk Chocolate to America

By Tziporah Cohen

Illustrated by Steven Salerno

CLARION BOOKS
AN IMPRINT OF HARPERCOLLINSPUBLISHERS

At the corner of Chocolate Avenue and Cocoa Avenue lives a story.

A story that began more than one hundred and fifty years ago.

A story about chocolate, though Milton Hershey probably never tasted chocolate as a child.

Chocolate was an expensive treat for the rich in the 1860s. Milton's family was very poor. His belly was often empty and his feet were often bare.

Milton Hershey in 1865
Age 8

On market day, Milton looked longingly at the displays of treats—sugarplums, molasses puffs, peanut brittle, peppermint humbugs, Peerless Wafers, horehound sticks!

Because his family moved often, Milton attended six schools in seven years and barely learned to read. When he was fourteen, he left school to help support his family.

Apprenticed to a printer, Milton hated the loud and boring work. So he threw his hat into the printing press to get himself fired!

At Royer's Ice Cream Parlor and Garden, Milton washed dishes and stirred big cauldrons of boiling sugar water. When he was promoted, he learned to make ice cream, taffy, lollipops, and marshmallows.

Candy made people happy.

Candy made *Milton* happy.

How wonderful would it be to
build his own candy business?

At nineteen, Milton borrowed money to open the Spring Garden Confectionery Works in Philadelphia, about one hundred miles from his home.

But the price of sugar was high and profits were low.

After six years, his business failed.

Milton Hershey in 1876
Age 19

Philadelphia

FAILED

At the time, sugar was made from the sugarcane plant and produced mainly in the Caribbean islands. Sugarcane was difficult to plant and harvest, leading to high prices. Years later, sugar would also be made from sugar beets in Europe and America, and its price would drop.

Next, Milton opened a candy business

further away, in Chicago.

It failed.

Chicago

FAILED

He opened one in the biggest city in America—New York City.

That one failed too.

It was time to go home.

New York

FAILED

But Milton loved candy too much to give up.

In a small rented room back in Pennsylvania, he cooked caramels.

He wrapped them by hand and sold them from a pushcart through the streets of Lancaster.

Oh, those tricky caramels! Other candymakers used wax in their caramels, but they were hard to chew and stuck to people's teeth.

Milton did experiment after experiment, adding fresh milk to make his caramels creamy but not sticky, until he got the recipe just right.

He cooked up all kinds of caramels:

Bean-shaped McGinties—a penny for ten.

Fancy Lotus caramels—a dollar for a five-pound box.

Jim Cracks and Roly Polys—caramels for every taste and every budget.

His rented room became a factory.

His pushcart became a store.

LANCASTER CARAMEL CO

China

Australia

LANCASTER

Milton realized that the secret to making money from caramels was not to peddle them a few at a time to people walking by, but to sell them in big shipments to stores in other cities and countries.

The store became the Lancaster Caramel Company.

Soon Milton was selling his caramels to stores in England, China, and Australia.

Milton Hershey in 1893
Age 36

Despite his success, Milton looked for new ways to make candy.

ZWILLINGSKAKAOMÜHLE
TWIN CACAO GRINDER

MISCHMASCHINE
MIXER

ENTLUFTUNGSMASCHINE
DEAERATION MACHINE

KLOPFTISCH
KNOCKING TABLE

WALZMASCHINE
ROLLING MACHINE

KAKAORÖSTMASCHINE
CACAO ROASTING MACHINE

BRECH
CRUSHI

At the Chicago World's Fair, he followed his nose.

Oh, the mouthwatering aroma of melted chocolate!

The chocolate-making machines from Germany mesmerized Milton.

He bought the whole exhibit on the spot and shipped it to Pennsylvania.

The very next year, Milton founded the Hershey Chocolate Company.

He told his cousin, "The caramel business is a fad. But chocolate is something we will always have."

Milton had a new vision:

Could he create delicious *milk* chocolate—in bars, just for eating?

Affordable milk chocolate—for everyone, not just the rich?

Milton headed back to the family farm.

He mixed chocolate made from cacao beans grown all over the world with milk from dairy cows raised right next door.

He stared at the burnt mush.

Milton saw that the chocolate, which was high in fat, couldn't mix with the milk, which was mostly water. Making milk chocolate made cooking caramels seem easy.

Milton worked from sunup to sundown.

He stirred big kettles of milk and sugar for hours, in search of the perfect recipe.

When he heated the milk to evaporate some of the water, the chocolate tasted burnt.

For thousands of years in Central and South America, chocolate was consumed mostly as a bitter drink. When solid dark chocolate was first made in Europe in the 1800s, it was expensive and mostly a treat for the wealthy. Then Nestlé invented milk chocolate in Switzerland, but it was still handmade and expensive. And the process was a secret that the Swiss had kept for more than twenty years!

When he used cream instead of milk, the chocolate
didn't harden well and spoiled quickly.

Milton even changed the kind of cows he raised
to ones that gave milk with less fat.

That helped, though the chocolate wasn't yet perfect.

HOLSTEIN
3.65%

AYRSHIRE
3.86%

BROWN
SWISS
4.04%

He hired scientists.

He hired workers from chocolate companies in Europe to try to learn their secrets.

Cook and cool.

Test and taste.

Milton and his staff worked day and night on his milk chocolate recipe.

YEARS went by.

Batch after **batch**,

one failure after another,

until, *finally* . . .

Milton Hershey in 1900
Age 43

HERSHEY
RECIPE
193

. . . America's first chocolate bar!

A melt-in-your-mouth milk chocolate.

A milk chocolate that stayed fresh on store shelves.

Milton sold the first Hershey's Bar in 1900. He also
sold the Lancaster Caramel Company—for one million
dollars—so he could make more milk chocolate.

Instead of making his chocolate bars by hand, Milton set up assembly lines in his factory, which divided each step among many workers to make chocolate bars more quickly.

With assembly lines, Milton made his milk chocolate affordable for everyone—just five cents a bar!

He put his chocolate bars in restaurants, drugstores, and grocery stores—not just candy stores—so people could buy them wherever they went.

just 5¢

Milk from local cows arrived at the factory daily, where workers combined it with sugar and chocolate, mixed it for four days, and then poured it into bar-shaped molds.

Within a few years, the Hershey Chocolate Company
had a factory running six days a week.

Kiss

The Hershey's Kiss was born in 1907, named for the kissing sound the drops of chocolate made as they were released onto the conveyor belt.

Sold in boxes for just ten cents, the foil-wrapped chocolate was an instant hit.

Hershey's Syrup was a sensation too. First made for pharmacists to add to bitter medicines to make them taste better, Milton sold chocolate syrup in cans for families to stir into milk or pour over ice cream.

Not everything Milton tried was a success. In the 1930s, vitamins were discovered. Milton joined the country's vitamin craze, mixing ground beets, celery, parsley, and turnips into Hershey's Bars and Kisses. One of his employees said that they "tasted just about as bad as they sound."

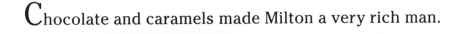

Chocolate and caramels made Milton a very rich man.

But he never forgot what it was like to be poor.

He and his wife, Catherine, created a school to give orphaned boys a free education, something he had never had.

HERSHEY →

He built an entire town for his workers to live in, with tree-lined streets, libraries, schools, trolleys, a swimming pool, affordable homes, and . . .

Milton and his wife never had children of their own, but they founded the Hershey Industrial School (now called the Milton Hershey School). Later, Milton donated his share of his company—worth sixty million dollars— to the school, so its mission to give kids in need a free education would continue indefinitely.

. . . even **a carousel!**

And today, if you stand on the corner of Chocolate Avenue and Cocoa Avenue—the first two streets Milton built—you can still smell the sweet scent of chocolate from the Hershey chocolate factory as it churns out milk chocolate for you, me, and chocolate lovers everywhere.

**Milton, age sixteen, apprentice at Royer's
Ice Cream Parlor and Garden**

Milton at age thirty
"One is only happy in proportion as he
makes others feel happy."
—Milton Hershey

Milton Hershey with some of the students at the Hershey Industrial School
Now known as the Milton Hershey School, the school provides a free education to more
than 2,000 boys and girls a year from lower-income families, from kindergarten to twelfth
grade, all thanks to the generosity of Milton Hershey and his wife, Catherine.

Source Notes

"The caramel business is a fad": D'Antonio, *Hershey: Milton S. Hershey's Extraordinary Life*, 69.

"tasted just about as bad as they sound": D'Antonio, *Hershey: Milton S. Hershey's Extraordinary Life*, 225.

"One is only happy in proportion": The Hershey Company. "Milton Hershey: The Man." (www .thehersheycompany.com/en_us/our-story/milton-hershey/the-man.html; accessed May 12, 2021)

Bibliography

Brenner, Joël G. *The Emperors of Chocolate: Inside the Secret World of Hershey and Mars*. New York: Random House, 1999.

Coe, Sophie D., and Michael D. Coe. *The True History of Chocolate*. London: Thames & Hudson, 2013.

D'Antonio, Michael. *Hershey: Milton S. Hershey's Extraordinary Life of Wealth, Empire, and Utopian Dreams*. New York: Simon & Schuster, 2006.

Frydenborg, Kay. *Chocolate: Sweet Science and Dark Secrets of the World's Favorite Treat*. Boston: Houghton Mifflin Harcourt, 2015.

Green, Hardy. *The Company Town: The Industrial Edens and Satanic Mills that Shaped the American Economy*. New York: Basic Books, 2010.

Hershey Community Archives. www.hersheyarchives.org.

Janik, Rachel. "How the Hershey's Kiss Conquered Valentine's Day." *Time,* Feb. 14, 2015. (www.time .com/3707086/hershey-kiss-history-valentines)

Wei-Haas, Maya. "The Unlikely Medical History of Chocolate Syrup." *Smithsonian* magazine, Sept. 6, 2017. (www.smithsonianmag.com/science-nature/unlikely-medical-history-chocolate-syrup-180964779)

To learn more about Milton Hershey:

Biography.com. "Milton Hershey." Apr. 27, 2017. (www.biography.com/people/milton-hershey)

Buckley, James, Jr. *Who Was Milton Hershey?* Illustrated by Ted Hammond. New York: Scholastic, 2014.

Eboch, M. M. *Milton Hershey: Young Chocolatier*. Illustrated by Meryl Henderson. New York: Aladdin Paperbacks, 2008.

Gillis, Jennifer B. *Milton Hershey: The Founder of Hershey's Chocolate*. Chicago: Heinemann Library, 2005.

The Hershey Company. "Milton Hershey." (www.thehersheycompany.com/en_us/our-story/milton-hershey.html; accessed May 12, 2021)

To learn more about chocolate:

Burleigh, Robert. *Chocolate: Riches from The Rainforest*. New York: Harry N. Abrams, 2002.

Frydenborg, Kay. *Chocolate: Sweet Science and Dark Secrets of the World's Favorite Treat*. Boston: Houghton Mifflin Harcourt, 2015.

Polin, C. J. *The Story of Chocolate*. New York: DK Children, 2005.

National Confectioners Association. "The Story of Chocolate." (www.thestoryofchocolate.com; accessed May 12, 2021)

Milton Hershey Timeline

1857 Milton Snavely Hershey is born in Derry Township, Pennsylvania, to parents Henry Hershey and Veronica "Fanny" Snavely.

1862 Milton's sister, Serina, is born.

1867 Serina dies of scarlet fever.

1869 Milton leaves school.

1871 Milton begins an apprenticeship with Samuel Ernest, a newspaper printer in Lancaster, Pennsylvania. He gets fired after a few months.

1872 Milton begins an apprenticeship with Lancaster candymaker Joe Royer at Royer's Ice Cream Parlor and Garden.
Milton's parents separate. He lives with his mother in Lancaster.

1876 Milton starts his own candy business in Philadelphia.

1882 The business in Philadelphia fails. Milton goes to Denver, Colorado, where he learns to make caramels with milk rather than paraffin (a type of wax).

1882–86 Milton opens businesses in Chicago and New York City, which both fail.

1886 Milton moves back to Lancaster and starts making caramels in a one-room workshop. He founds the Lancaster Caramel Company.

1893 Milton buys chocolate-making equipment at the Chicago World's Fair (the World's Columbian Exposition) and ships it back home to Lancaster.

1894 The Hershey Chocolate Company is founded.

1898 Milton marries Catherine "Kitty" Sweeney in St. Patrick's Cathedral in New York City.

1900 Milton sells the Lancaster Caramel Company for one million dollars.
The first Hershey's Milk Chocolate Bar is sold.

1903 Milton breaks ground on his new factory and the town that will become Hershey, Pennsylvania. Chocolate Avenue and Cocoa Avenue are the first streets that Hershey builds.

1909 With Kitty, Milton founds the Hershey Industrial School, later renamed the Milton Hershey School.

1915 Kitty dies.

1918 Milton donates his entire fortune of sixty million dollars to the Hershey Industrial School.

1926 Hershey's Chocolate Syrup is sold in stores, to make chocolate milk at home.

1945 Milton Hershey dies at age eighty-eight in Hershey, Pennsylvania.

For Dad (Special Dark) and Jay (Milk Chocolate with Almonds) —**T.C.**

For Tita, Arturo, Christina, and Sofia —**S.S.**

Clarion Books is an imprint of HarperCollins Publishers. • On the Corner of Chocolate Avenue • Text copyright © 2022 by Tziporah Cohen • Illustrations copyright © 2022 by Steven Salerno • All rights reserved. Manufactured in Italy. No part of this book may be used or reproduced in any manner whatsoever without written permission except in the case of brief quotations embodied in critical articles and reviews. For information address HarperCollins Children's Books, a division of HarperCollins Publishers, 195 Broadway, New York, NY 10007. • www.harpercollinschildrens.com • ISBN 978-0-35-857875-8 • The artist used Photoshop, combining digital drawings with gouache painted textures, to create the illustrations for this book. • Typography by Samira Iravani • 22 23 24 25 26 RTLO 10 9 8 7 6 5 4 3 2 1 • First Edition